# E- Commerce for Traditional African Attires

# (A Business Idea)

# By

# Jack Lookman

**Gratitude:**

Ogo ni fun Olorun

All Gratitude to Allah.

Alhamdulillah

To God Be the Glory

Soli Deo gloria

Gratitude as well, to my parents, my family, my teachers, all loved ones and to all journey partners.

**Dedication:**

To all those who travail difficult life sojourns.

May your difficulties be eased.

Ire O.

Jack Lookman

www.jacksinspiration.com

Youtube Channel: Jack Lookman

Facebook Group: Emowerment, Inspiration and Support

Our goal is to empower and inspire generations

# About Jack Lookman

Real name is Olayinka Carew.

He resides in the UK and is an Interpreneur and owner of Jack Lookman Limited.

He studied Engineering in University, but stopped practicing since the mid-1990's.

He considers himself creative and has lots of business ideas to share. In his earlier years, sometime between 1975- 1980, the idea of a flying car came to mind while he was stuck in road traffic. This partly influenced his going into Engineering.

Life's twists and turns caused a change in direction.

Ill health, relocation, and a different calling have manifested in this disposition.

He has varied work experience in different industries, but his long-term goal is to empower and inspire generations.

His outlets in impacting communities, are via social media, writing, blogging, vlogging, and hopefully soon, via public speaking.

He has authored different books and has also worked in different voluntary roles.

He is blessed with an aged mum, 4 siblings and 3 children.

May Allah grant my deceased father Aljannah Firdaus.

Whereas some may view life's challenges as negative and difficult; these are the springboards with which he hopes to soar and achieve.

# About Jack Lookman Limited

Our mission is to empower and inspire generations by leveraging the internet.

We use social media extensively and have presences in the underlisted platforms:

Our YouTube Channel is 'Jack Lookman'

Our Facebook Group is 'Empowerment, Inspiration and Support'.

Our Blog is 'www.jacksinspiration.com'.

Our content ranges from business ideas, mindset issues to sharing life experiences and other topics that help us fulfil our mission.

The company was registered in 2015 and is based in the United Kingdom.

We have also authored a few books, which are available on Amazon.com and other outlets.

# Inspiration for this book

Being a British- Nigerian based in the UK, there is sometimes the need to dress in African traditional attire.

This is usually a logistic challenge and could prove expensive.

Rather than lament all day long, the thought occurred to me to begin the value chain by sharing my thoughts as well as the opportunities.

I have a lot to share, following my varied life experience and exposure.

In my paid and unpaid work; in my formal and informal education, in my ups and downs in life; throughout my existence; there have been lots of lessons.

I am opportuned to have a great education. I have lots of wisdom and life experience. I also have creative ideas that could benefit those who wish to take these further.

My strength is my creativity; not as a musician or artist; but as an entrepreneur. I generally see opportunity in most situations, even in adversity.

Those who have a strength in execution are most welcome to collaborate or take the ideas to the next level.

I have waited for so long to unleash my thoughts and ideas.
God has created that opportunity. I am now exploring it.

# Index

28. What are the cost implications?
29. Start-up assets
30. Initial start-up costs
31. Fixed costs
32. Running costs
33. Create a spreadsheet
34. Fill in your predicted business activity
35. Predicted revenue generation
36. Break-even point
37. Add sunk costs
38. Should you consider a partnership or a joint venture?
39. Decide the roles and responsibilities of each partner
40. Determine a profit-sharing formula
41. Insert an exit clause
42. Determine how to handle a dissolution
43. Registering your business name
44. Going with the business structure
45. Going with DBA
46. Trademarking your business
47. Business plan
48. Executive summary
49. Opportunity
50. Buyer avatar/ persona
51. Product research/ knowledge
52. Unique selling point
53. Competitor matrix
54. Future products and services
55. Execution
56. Target marketing and sales plan

57. Pricing
58. Promotion
59. Packaging
60. Advertising
61. Content marketing
62. Affiliate marketing
63. Social media
64. Strategic alliances
65. Business consultants
66. Operations
67. Technology
68. Fulfilment/ cloth material
69. Stocking/ peculiarities
70. Distribution/ courier
71. Key assumptions, risks and external factors
72. Company management and summary
73. Team
74. Location
75. Intellectual property
76. Legal structure
77. Financial plan
78. Personnel plan
79. Resource management/ cash flow statement
80. Refund policy and bogus customers
81. Exit strategy
82. Appendix
83. Branding
84. Logo
85. Personality

# 1. INTRODUCTION

E-commerce is an avenue through which commerce is generated by leveraging the internet. There are different e-commerce stores in the marketplace. Examples include Amazon and Shopify. Products come at different prices and the sites have common and different features.

In the last decade, e-commerce has experienced exponential growth globally, becoming such an important facet of daily living. Presently, about 22% of the world's population shops online. Still, many projections indicate further growth, with one asserting that retail e-commerce sales may reach $5 trillion by 2021. The coronavirus pandemic will only hasten the realisation of these projections. Individuals, small businesses and big companies have had to turn to e-commerce to keep the supply chain going. Retail platforms experienced an unprecedented increase in global traffic between January 2019 and June 2020, surpassing even holiday season peaks. This surge indicates that there is a place for you in e-commerce. All you need is a sound business idea, an agile business plan and meticulous implementation.

One business idea you should consider is African attire retailing. Africa is home to a plethora of colourful fabrics. There's the Akwete cloth and Ukara dyed indigo cloth by Igbo people; Aso oke fabric and Adire tie-dye created by Yoruba people; Kente cloth produced by the Buganda tribe; Mudcloth produced by the Bambara tribe; Shweshwe and Kitenge produced by South Africa, Kenya and other East African Regions. Throw in Ankara fabrics into this and what you have is a diverse mix capable of drawing buyers from anywhere in the world. Ankara fabrics became one of the most sought-after fabrics in the world because of their stunning beauty and versatility. They are so versatile that you can conveniently use them for almost any style, retro or contemporary. Ankara fabrics can be used to make iro, buba, gowns, suits, skirts, swimsuits, blazers, hats, earrings, kaftans, blouse, jumpsuits, and aso ebi--loosely translated as "clothes of the family." If you do decide to go into the African attire business, there would be no shortage of fabrics or styles for your buyers.

## 2. Overview

This business idea is about selling packaged African attires via e-commerce to Africans at home and in the diaspora.

You'll get supplies of African attires in bulk from more than one supplier to encourage diversity in your stock. You will then produce different styles with different materials, guided by specifications like height and body size, as well as trends. Properly packaged, you'll then retail these to your customers via e-commerce. You will be doing what western shops do with western clothes. The difference is that this will be for African attires. Your sales could be in Africa and, or the diaspora.

## 3. How is this better than going to a traditional tailor?

The main difference between this value proposition and going to the regular tailor is that you could place your order from the comfort of your home and get your outfit delivered to you within a couple of days. You don't need to purchase materials or make any journeys, plus you don't have to deal with some tailors' unreliability. Once you get the sizes and materials right, it's as good as done.

## 4. How will you go about sourcing your stock?

Africa has a long history of textile production. Where you source your stock will depend on several factors such as price, availability, quality, delivery, and minimum order quantity. Since 1845, Vlisco has designed and manufactured over 350,000 prints inspired by Africa, utilising the technique adopted from Indonesian Batik in Netherland. You could source for Wax Holland, Java and Super Wax from them. You could also source from the Rughani Brothers, manufacturer and exporter of African fabrics. They have a collection of fabrics with vibrant colours, unique styles and traditional patterns.

However, if you're looking to source from a Western or Asian company, you could try Yara African Fabrics, Aaron International or Qingdao Phoenix. Yara is based in New York and boasts a collection of unique African patterns and colours, including African Gold Prints, Batik and Tie-Dye Fabric, Graphic Print, Kente Print, Mudcloth Print, Patchwork, Vegetable Print, and Wax Prints. While the US-based Aaron International produces and supplies African laces, fabrics, wax prints, head-ties, and guipure blouse. Qingdao Phoenix is a China-based company that manufactures and supplies African fabrics like soso, java, imitation wax, real wax, Indian blue block wax, pearl powder printing, and golden powder printing.

Interestingly, you could provoke suppliers into bidding by providing them with specifications, which would allow you the opportunity to use your judgment in selecting which of them serves your purpose best. You may try a few and have others as back up.

## 5. Should I source and produce in Africa?

This is going to depend on your location, budget, scope of your operations and target customers. For example, if you live somewhere in Africa and looking to sell within and outside Africa, then it makes sense to source materials from African manufacturers, produce your designs and package them in Africa. This takes away the cost of importation, plus the cost of producing African garments in Africa is much cheaper than doing so outside of Africa.

However, if you live in the UK for example, then it might make more sense to look for a manufacturer of African fabrics within the UK to avoid importation costs. Turning those materials into beautiful attires is indeed cheaper in Africa, but you might be better off looking for competent designers within the UK. You might have to pay a bit more money, but the cost of using designers in Africa and then paying to have your designs imported can offset the extra money you pay to work with designers in the UK.

As for exporting your designs to reach foreign buyers, you need to make financial and logistical considerations. If reaching foreign customers isn't financially viable at the beginning, consider focusing on local buyers and then expand when you're ready.

## 6. Quality control

First and foremost, you need to give clear specifications of your requirements to your suppliers. You also need to have a written contract or agreement with them, preferably with witnesses. You could have quality control checks by appointed 3rd parties who work in that trade. They could do spot checks on the products before they are shipped to you. The quality controller should be someone of impeccable character who will not be bought over by the supplier. There will also be contracts with the quality controller.

To reduce costs, the controller could be engaged for a few hours weekly or monthly, or as necessary, to carry out that function and there could be legal implications for defaults.

## 7. Would there be expansion opportunities?

The good thing about starting a business is that there will usually be other opportunities. Some of these opportunities present themselves in the course of the business while others could come as a result of others wanting to partner with you or through suggestions by others. Much as this may be beneficial, be careful not to lose focus.

The versatility of African fabrics means that there would be multiple expansion opportunities. African fabrics can be used to make caps, headgears, belts, phone covers, bags, shoes, ties, bow ties, watch straps, jewellery like earrings, necklaces, bangles, and just about anything. However, master what you do first before exploring wider business opportunities. Doing too much at once from the beginning might affect you adversely.

## 8. Cross-selling

Cross-selling is simply the act of identifying products that serve complementary purposes not provided by the original item being purchased. So when the time comes for you to expand, consider starting with products that complement African attires. Examples of such products include shoes, watches, caps, ties and bow ties, and glasses, all of them made with an African print design. This would easily encourage your customers to come to you for their complete outfits and accessories so that they don't have to order from different online retailers. You will also be leveraging the trust and relationship built with your customers.

### 9. Why Are You Sharing This Idea?

I am part of the value chain. I believe that by playing my part and sharing the idea, it could add value to the populace, create jobs, create wealth, create convenience for the customer, reduce crime, improve the economy and other potential benefits.

### 10.    Why Should I Pursue This Business Idea?

Besides its lucrativeness, the versatility of African attires, combined with the fact that clothes will always be in demand, makes this business idea an attractive one. Additionally, you would be creating opportunities for other people through the team you would employ, which would include designers, couriers, staff and strategists. Your tailors would be busy and fully engaged. They would have a regular source of income and could aspire to greater things. Also, you'd be contributing to the growth of your country's economy by extension. Job creation has far-reaching effects like crime reduction and bigger tax returns.

Secondly, with technology, the whole world has become a global village. You get to take advantage of the wider reach and ease of distribution that technology offers at a lower cost. For your customers, this translates to greater comfort and efficiency, allowing them to quickly place specific orders and have the items delivered to their doorstep within a week. And with the variety of designs, colours, materials, styles and sizes on your e-commerce site, your customers would always be spoilt for choice.

## 11. Requirements

There are tangible and intangible requirements that would come in handy right from the inception of your business down to day to day operations. Stock management is one of the skills you want to have because it can impact sales and your overall finances. Your stock management skills allow you to make astute predictions of market demand. You can predict when demand for certain attire falls and when it might rise again, allowing you to stock up accordingly.

However, you don't have to singularly embody all these requirements because it's practically impossible to do that. To start and successfully run the business, the following would be required:

- Business capital
- Resource management skills
- Project management skills
- Time management skills
- Communication skills

- Data management
- Problem-solving skills
- Market knowledge
- Organisational skills
- Stock management skills
- Analytical skills
- Customer Services Skills
- People Management Skills
- Fraud Management Skills
- Computer Skills

Fortunately, there are a lot of apps out there you can invest in to help you with management. All you need to do is search Google. Also, most of the above skills can be learned if you are lacking in any area. There are business management courses on Udemy and Skillshare. You can also read articles and watch expert videos on YouTube. Below are the values and best practices you might want to aspire to:

12.     **Trust:** Customers need to trust that they'd get quality outfits that are carefully designed. This means that you have to be careful where you source your stock and the designers you employ. Bad experiences stay with customers and that can affect your brand equity.

13.     **Reliability and integrity:** If a customer expects their delivery in three days, try and deliver in three days. This communicates to the customer that you're reliable. Don't give a delivery timeline you wouldn't meet. If something unexpected

disrupts your process, communicate this to your customer and maybe even come up with a token as redress.

14.     **Good customer service:** Ensure that your customer service is great. That way, you'll not only have happy customers, but they'll end up marketing your brand for free. A solid refund policy goes a long way in letting customers know that if something goes wrong, they can get their money back.

15.     **How To Conduct Your Market Research**

Before thrusting yourself into the African attire business, it is very important to conduct comprehensive market research to gain adequate knowledge of the market. This research would help you answer some pertinent questions, allowing you to decide on the feasibility of this business venture. You should be able to answer the following questions after conducting the research:

- Is your product in demand?
- Can customers afford it?
- Will they pay for it?
- How large is your target market?
- Could you make a profit?
- What is different about your proposition?
- Is competition high, low or somewhere in-between?
- What are the strengths and weaknesses of your competition?
- Are there governmental restrictions that can affect your business?

Here are seven steps on how to conduct a comprehensive market assessment:

### 16.    Decide on the purpose of your study

Market research is conducted for different purposes. It can be used to assess risks, create opportunities, analyse past and future success. So you need to decide whether the research is for internal or external purposes or both. This would help determine the scope of the research, the amount of data to be collected, and precisely where to focus resources.

### 17.    Analyse the outlook of your industry

Analysing your industry would help you understand the current state of the industry, where it is headed and what the projected growth is. This would help you answer the question of whether the African attire industry would still be buzzing in the next decade or so.

### 18.    Locate your target customers

The next step is to pinpoint your target customers. You need to have a robust understanding of their personas. Who are they? Where do they come from? Where do they belong on the income spectrum? Use metrics like age, income, gender, education, occupation and marital status.

### 19.    Analyse your competition

Analysing your competition helps you understand what they offer, their location, their mode of operation, their target customers and the overall disadvantages of the market. Try answering these questions: Are they a threat to your business? Why would a customer go to them instead of you? In what area do they have the advantage? What can you do better?

20.    **Collect more data**

Collect as much data as you can. Data is the backbone of your entire market analysis, so don't hesitate to collect loads of it. However, the data you collect should be relevant and factual, which means using credible sources like state and commerce websites, articles in trade journals, the census bureau and bureau of labour statistics.

21.    **Evaluate your findings**

The next thing is to evaluate your findings by organising them into sections like competition, target market and purpose. Your findings should include your outlook of the African attire industry, buying trends, price and discount offerings, projected growth, market percentage and customers' price range.

22.    **Put your analysis to work**

This is the time to start putting your analysis into action. A lot of work goes into arriving at this point of actionable intelligence, but it is very important if your business is to put a strong foot forward. Additionally, if you happen to need external funding to go into the African attire business, investors would want to look at it and know that you have done your homework.

23.    **Choosing A Niche**

The market research you've conducted would go a long way in helping you decide on a niche. You already have a comprehensive idea of the African attire market at this point. You know what the market has to offer, its advantages and disadvantages. You know the problems you want to solve, the profitability and pitfalls. And you know your competition, their strengths and weaknesses. Whether you want to target a particular age range, specific geographic locations, Africans or lovers of African wear, men or women or both, depends on you and what your market research is telling you to do.

However, if you're still not quite certain where to settle in, here a few suggestions:

24.    **Kids:** Every parent wants to see their kid(s) looking good wherever they go. Most parents put more into clothing their kids than they do for themselves. Whether to target African parents in the diaspora or just parents who are big fans of African attire in your country of residence would depend on your market research.

25.    **Aso ebi:** The aso ebi culture is prevalent amongst the Yorubas in southwest Nigeria. The concept is shared in some other cultures. It is one where close family or friends use the same materials for different designs and then wear them like 'uniform(s)' as a show of support for the hosts of the event. As a business, you could leverage this by supplying the garments accordingly.

26.    **Parties:** Africans, especially Nigerians, love parties. They dress flamboyantly and are very fashionable. This plays very well to the business proposition. You might choose to leverage this need

or opportunity and make as much money as possible by delivering products and services to satisfy their wants and needs.

27.    **Cultural get-togethers:** The African people are generally colourful and sometimes flamboyant and fashionable. They have deep cultural heritages, which are celebrated at different times of the year. One example is the August Meeting celebrated by the Igbo women of eastern Nigeria. Interestingly, Africans in the diaspora hardly abandon these culturally significant days wherever they are in the world. This fits very well into business prospects and longevity.

28.    **What Are The Cost Implications?**

Every business requires funding. Whether you intend to take a loan, find investors or fund it out of your pocket is another matter. Regardless, you need to know the full cost implication of starting this business. This knowledge will be crucial in figuring out whether you can afford to fund the business or to look for external funding. It would also play a big part in the determination of the prices of your products.

Sometimes, there tend to be misunderstandings when it comes to the scope of start-up financing and its calculation. When you're looking to calculate the cost implication of starting the African attire business, it should account for how much money the entire thing needs up until the moment the business starts making profits of its own. Your calculation should cover the initial start-up costs (business registration, legal fees), assets purchase (e-commerce site, stock, branding) and the running costs of opening the business itself (salaries, logistics, administration, interest payable by loans, miscellaneous expenses and other utilities). To effectively account for all costs, you will need to make a financial forecast of the business. Follow the template below:

29. **Start-up assets:** Any assets you think you'll need to buy for the African attire business, list all of them. Afterwards, check retail stores online for the cost of each item to know how much to fill in as the cost.

30. **Initial start-up costs:** Create a list of the initial start-up costs, including registration, branding, e-commerce web hosting and set up. If there are any recurring costs, you should also put it on the list.

31. **Fixed costs:** Fixed costs are those that remain fixed and are to be incurred over a specific period. It doesn't matter whether your business is making a profit or not, fixed costs must continue to be paid. Make a list of any cost that falls under this category.

32. **Running costs:** Running costs, as the name implies, refers to the cost of running the business until it starts yielding profit. Costs that vary and are linked to how much sales you're able to make should also be listed.

After making the above list and finding out the costs, the next thing you need to do is create a business forecast. Follow the template below:

33. **Create a spreadsheet:** List your sunk costs including assets and initial expenses and calculate the total. The sunk cost is the amount of money that funds your business up to the point it gets launched.

34. **Fill in your predicted business activity:** Predicted business activity is the fixed cost of running the business. In the same

spreadsheet, fill in the fixed amount you would spend on electricity, broadband, rent, salaries and other utilities for the length of 12 months at least.

35.     **Predicted revenue generation:** The next thing is to model your price, the number of customers you might serve each month, variable costs and revenue for each month. For each month, subtract your variable costs (electricity, logistics, staffing) and fixed costs from the revenue generated that same month. In the end, the result will show a profit or loss.

36.     **Break-even point:** Here, you need to calculate the number of customers you need to serve each month for your business to start making profits. Naturally, the months you tried to account for above would generate losses for which you took a sum. That would help you work out how many products to sell before you can take home a profit.

37.     **Add sunk costs:** The final step is to add your sum cost to the cumulative loss totalled above. This would provide you with the total amount you'd need to finance the business up until you start making profits.

38.     **Should You Consider a Partnership or a Joint Venture?**

On successfully calculating the total amount of capital it would take to go into the African attire business, the next thing is to check your finances and decide whether you can finance the business all on your own or whether you need help. If indeed you need help, there are a few ways to share the costs such as entering a joint venture with a friend, relative or partner, business angel, crowdfunding, taking a loan from a bank, or looking for external investors.

However, a partnership and a joint venture are quite different. A joint venture is when two or more people or entities join together for a specific project, while a partnership involves two individuals joining together for a combined business. In a partnership, the parties involved agree to share the profits as well as any loss incurred in a single venture. Nonetheless, both have some moving parts you need to understand before making your choice. Here are a few things to consider when entering a partnership:

### 39.   Decide the roles and responsibilities of each partner

As a way to manage expectations and avoid resentment, every partner should have their roles and responsibilities cut out for them. You don't want to have a situation where one partner feels cheated because they believe that they put in more effort into the business than another partner. All the partners should sit down and decide what their obligations would be based on what's best for the growth of the business. These roles and responsibilities could be reviewed as necessary.

### 40.   Determine a profit-sharing formula

The two main factors to be considered when entering a partnership are the responsibility and capital contributions. All the partners would have to come together and decide how the profits and losses would be shared. This should be done based on the terms of the agreement. However, if the two parties are close, some prefer to go in blind without an agreement. You will need to give this some thought to ensure that you don't shoot yourself in the foot.

### 41.   Insert an exit clause

Partnership or joint venture, whichever you decide to go with, ensure that there is an exit clause for when your vision or strategic interests no longer align. Any of the partners is always free to leave anytime and the clause comes into effect immediately. Every partnership ends at some point, due to unforeseen circumstances and sometimes not. So don't feel that by bringing up the exit clause to your partners you're already thinking the business would fail.

## 42.    Determine how to handle a dissolution

When it's time to dissolve the partnership, tempers might run high or not. To prepare for this scenario, you need to determine how each partner would be compensated and how resources would be divided. When it's time to split, all the partners would defer to the operating agreement already signed from the beginning.

## 43.    Registering Your Business Name

Your business name is a matter of choice and different countries and states have different guidelines on how to register a business name. Some states let you register online while some only conduct in-person registration. As far as registering your business name goes, you have three options to choose from, which include registering your business structure and operating under that name, filing for a 'Do Business As' (DBA) or trademarking your business name. Each of these could be chosen for slightly different reasons explained below:

## 44.    Going with the business structure

This option allows you to register your business name at the state level, ensuring that the name is officially yours and that you can do business using that name. This option is considered to be the most straightforward if you're looking to register a partnership or LLC. All you need to do is register the structure.

## 45. Going with DBA

As mentioned above, you can just register your structure and get on with doing business under the name. However, if you want to change the name of the structure under which your business is registered, you can simply apply for a DBA. Most people do this because they want to use a name that is part of their business identity.

## 46. Trademarking your business

Another way to register your business is to trademark it, at the state and national level if you so choose. Consider trademarking your business if you're looking for something that covers not just the name but your business slogans, logos, colours, and symbols.

## 47. Business Plan

The market research you've done comes in handy here. You don't need an MBA for this, so don't be intimidated by it. You can find simple templates online to guide you. Your business plan should be as brief and concise as possible. A good business plan consists of six parts: executive summary, opportunity, execution and operation, company and management summary, financial plan and appendix.

## 48.    Executive summary

This should come last in the business plan, though some people prefer to write it first. This part captures what type of company you are and what you do. This is a summary of the entire business plan, so you need to know your business inside out. Your market research helps.

## 49.    Opportunity

This section covers the problem you're solving, the solution your product provides, who you're offering them to and how they fit into the market. This is your chance to show what makes you different from your competition and how you plan to expand in the future. Here are a few other things to figure out under opportunity:

50.    **Buyer avatar/persona:** You need to have a fully realised picture of the buyer such that you can see them clearly when you close your eyes. Are they younger or older citizens or both? Are they Africans in the diaspora? Are they working class? Are they upper class, family units? This is very important for other strategies such as marketing, content production, advertising and promotion.

51.    **Product research/knowledge:** Detail your knowledge of the African attires and the materials. As a business person, you need to know the intricacies of your business. Will the attires be machine washable? Under what conditions should they be washed and ironed? Could the attires be washed with others? Will the colours stain other clothes? Will materials shrink if washed under certain conditions? Are there peculiar problems in the countries of

import, such as poor electricity supply, poor productivity and poor attitude in general?

52.     **Unique selling point:** This is where you put down the things that make your business unique for your customer. You're saving customers time and the stress of having to deal with tailors by taking on the responsibility and delivering to them. Simply put, your selling point is packaging African tailored attires via e-commerce.

53.     **Competitor matrix:** Most businesses use competitor matrix to track and compare their features against their competition. Even when your business is underway, you need to keep checking which African attire materials and styles are in vogue and the changing practices of your competition.

54.     **Future products and services:** Your vision for expansion in the future should come under this section. Every entrepreneur envisages a point where the business is big and strong enough for expansion. However, don't put too much energy into expanding on these ideas. A paragraph or two should do the job. Concentrate more on bringing your African attire to your target customers first.

55.     Execution

As the title suggests, this is where you'd write down how to bring the business to life. Below is a breakdown of everything that should come under execution:

56.     **Target marketing and sales plan:** This part is integral to execution. This covers your pricing plan, how you plan on delivering

to your target customers, and the partnerships you intend to get into to make the business successful. You can launch your e-commerce website, or use Amazon.com or Shopify.com.

57. **Pricing:** There are three ways to approach your pricing strategy. They include cost-plus pricing, market-based pricing and value-based pricing. For your start-up, the cost-plus pricing is the ideal model. Pricing is very critical. You need to ensure due diligence when it comes to pricing. If you get it right, your business could flourish. Otherwise, it might eventually go bust.

Pricing may vary from time to time depending on different variables that may be within or outside your control. You need to take into consideration factors like logistics, profit margin, cost of getting the product from the supplier, cost of storage, administrative costs, staffing costs, insurance, refunds, etc

58. **Promotion:** This section covers how you intend to approach promotion. This details the media you want to use for promotion and how you want your target market to perceive your brand. However, you should be able to gauge how much impact your promotion might have. You don't want to sink so much money into promotion while it brings only small or no returns.

59. **Packaging:** Packaging is important in business. To decide your packaging, you need to consider your value proposition, how it measures up to competition, and your positioning strategy.

60. **Advertising:** You need to decide which ad medium you want to use. Do you intend to use traditional offline media or online? Make sure you have a way of measuring the impact of your ads.

61.     **Content marketing:** This involves providing information (articles, copies, tips) that would help the customer journey. You want a Search Engine Optimisation (SEO) expert who can pull visitors to your site with highly optimised content. Creating content positions you as an expert in your industry, which helps boost sales.

62.     **Affiliate marketing:** If your business can accommodate it, you could get affiliate marketers on board. Each time they initiate sales, they get a percentage of your marketing budget. This process is usually automated with checks and balances in place.

63.     **Social media:** Your business needs to have a presence across social media. This doesn't mean you have to be on every single platform. You have to make a choice and put it down in the business plan.

64.     **Strategic alliances:** This involves the alliance you plan to make to push your products out there. If you intend to use social media influencers or project ambassadors who would help sample your attires, it needs to be in the plan.

65.     **Business consultants:** Starting a new business can be a very overwhelming venture, especially if you're doing it all on your own. It should be in the plan if you are considering bringing on a business consultant who would act as an expert guide. The consultant could give insights into best practices, funding, avoidance of pit holes, etc.

66.     **Operations**

This section covers how your business is going to operate daily. For your African attire start-up, here are a few things to account for under this section:

67. **Technology:** For the daily operations of your African attire business, you'd need the help of relevant technology to make things easier. You need to decide and indicate which ones to invest in. Examples include time and project management apps, communication channels and tools for collaboration.

68. **Fulfilment/cloth material:** You need to disclose the material being used for each garment and all the measurements associated with it. That way, you can effectively manage expectations. You could have different price ranges for different ranges of good quality garments and materials. All of this information should be on the plan so it can be made available to your website developer, who would then create the relevant sections.

69. **Stocking/peculiarities:** One peculiarity of the complete traditional attire is that the individual pieces are usually of the same material. It becomes difficult to have a one-size-fits-all. To mitigate this challenge, you may consider selling individual pieces. You may need to code your stock by material, colour, size, and what type of wear (trouser, top, gown, etc). Also, consider putting down something on how to regulate your stock according to seasons.

70. **Distribution/courier:** You need to figure out a model for your distribution. You may need to ask questions or interview others in the African attire industry to know the most efficient way to get your attires to your customers. This is a very important component of your business, so you need to engage a good courier service. Not getting that right could break your business, no matter how good

the product is. If you promise delivery within 2 days, ensure the customer gets it as promised. No ifs or buts or excuses. Your integrity is at stake and you could lose customers.

71.     **Key assumptions, risks and external factors**: No matter how much you plan, there are key assumptions you've made. There are  risks and external factors you can't always control. A recent example is COVID-19 which has caused most plans to tumble. Other possibilities are political decisions, armed robbery, logistics failures, power cuts and unrest in countries, etc. The important thing is that you do your best to mitigate against such eventualities.

Furthermore, political decisions may have a role to play in this business venture. The politicians in different locations may create measures or policies that may or may not benefit the industry, from time to time. Ensure that you factor such eventualities in this section of your business plan.

## 72.     Company management and summary

This where you key in the structure of the business, the team and other utility players. Below are some of the things to account for in this section:

73.     **Team**: Every business is only as good as the team behind it. So you must assemble the best team your start-up budget would allow and then expand the team as you grow. One of the most important team members is the designer. They are professionally

trained and could facilitate the process. Right from the design, to logistics, to stock management, to measurements, to quality control, etc.

Also, this section would go a long way to facilitate your hiring process. So you need to create mini-bios or profiles of the relevant skills every team member needs to have and whether you'll be investing in further skill acquisition. Can this team bring your idea to life? Do they have industry experience? What are their achievements? These are a few questions that would help you figure out the profiles of your prospective team members.

74.    **Location:** Even though you'll be using e-commerce to sell most of your products, your customers need to know if you have a physical location. This gives your customers the option of visiting your store for live purchases. However, if you haven't set up a physical location yet, you could skip this part.

75.    **Intellectual property:** This is where to indicate if you have any intellectual property or patents that are proprietary to your business. Owning your intellectual rights helps keep your competitors at bay. For example, if you think in the future you and your designer might come up with a design you want to patent, this is where you include the details.

76.    **Legal Structure:** You need to put some thought into deciding what your legal structure would be. In the course of establishing this business, there are a lot of contracts you'd have to enter. You need to be aware of your legal rights and responsibilities, to your employees and your business associates in all the countries impacted by your trade. If you are an employer of labour, you need

to abide by legal restrictions, come up with business policies that cover leave, sickness pay, parental leave, disputes, lateness, absence, disciplinary issues, etc.

## 77.    Financial Plan

Your financial plan should include sales and revenue forecasts, plus yearly projections for four to five years. This creates a picture of where your business is headed and where it might be in the next half-decade. This would also be important if you're sourcing for funding from investors. Below are a few things to consider under this section:

**78.    Personnel plan:** This is where you list the number of staff you might need to get the business off the ground and how you intend to pay their salaries. This is something you should adequately account for if you don't want to have unhappy staff in the first few months of the business. You should have a rough estimate you plan to pay each staff in each position.

Also, you need to include "employee burden," which includes the cost an employee might incur beyond what you pay them as salary. The employee burden should include insurance, payroll taxes and other incentivisation of stakeholders and staff.

**79.    Resource management/cash flow statement:** Even when your African attire business is off the ground, you have to have a good plan to manage cash flow and resources for the business to keep growing. A cash flow statement accounts first for the money you have in hand. Then when you make sales, add everything up and then deduct the taxes and all the cash you have paid out for salaries and other utilities. You end up with your actual cash flow.

80.    **Refund policy and bogus customers**: Refund policies help you determine when a refund is in order. You have a clear and non-negotiable idea of the circumstances under which a customer merits a refund and you need to make this clear. There will likely be some customers who will take advantage of the process.

They could purchase clothes for particular engagements, and then return them to you for one fake reason or the other. It's up to you to have a watertight refund policy. If you notice recurring patterns from any of your customers, you might consider flagging them. However, remember that customers are protected legally. Your refund policy should be within the law.

81.    **Exit strategy**: You need to have an exit strategy in your business plan in case you want to sell the business or go public with it. However, you can overlook this part if you plan to maintain sole ownership and have absolutely no intention of looking for angel investment.

82.    **Appendix**

This section of the business plan is expendable. But if you have tables, charts, legal notes, definitions and any other important information associated with starting and running your business, then this is the section for it.

83.    **Branding**

The importance of branding for your African attire business cannot be overstated. Branding is responsible for how your customers view your brand, helping attract more sales through the use of logos, symbols, colours, slogan and statements. Branding is what keeps you in the mind of your audience and distinguishes you and your product from your competition. A good brand creates trust, satisfaction, recognition and value. Below are the components that come together to create a strong brand identity:

84.    **Logo:** You need a competent graphic designer to create a logo that would represent your African attire business. You need to get this right from the onset because your business logo isn't something you can change at will. The graphic designer has to do a lot of research about African attire to have an idea of what your business is all about.

However, don't make the mistake of accepting a logo that simply follows existing trends. Your business would just blend in instead of standing out from your competition. So the graphic designer needs to come up with something original and simple enough to stick to people's minds after a few glances. To find freelance graphic designers, you could visit sites like Upwork.com, Fiverr.com, Peopleperhour.com, or Freelancer.com.

85.    **Personality:** Your brand personality is the emotional and personal qualities associated with your brand. This is especially important since this is an African attire business. Which emotion do you want people to think of when they remember your brand?

How do you want them to feel? Do you want them to think flamboyant? Elegant? Traditional? Trendy?

86.     **Colour:** 85% of customers believe that colour goes a long way in motivating them to patronise a particular brand. This tells you just how significant colour is to branding. Before settling on a particular colour(s), you need to understand what colour means, how customers respond to colour, where colours should appear, identify your brand essence, and check competitor brands. Your brand colour should be consistent across all channels.

87.     **Mission statement:** This is where you tell your target customers what you do in a concise and catchy way. A customer needs to have an idea of what you do the first time they look at your mission statement. Writing a mission statement is a bit tricky. You need to make it broad enough that it covers everything you do in case of future expansion. You don't want a mission statement that becomes redundant once you expand.

88.     **Equity:** Brand equity simply means brand value, determined by how customers perceive you through their experience with your brand. A good way to build brand equity is to under-promise and over-deliver instead of the other way round. If you are always disappointing your customers, you'd end up with negative brand equity. Positive brand equity builds awareness, customer loyalty and recognition. Getting positive brand equity is half the job, maintaining it is the other half.

89.     **How Can You Market on Amazon or Shopify?**

Amazon is a competitive marketplace, but if you can figure it out you can make substantial sales because lots of people shop there. With a conversion rate of roughly 15%, Amazon triples every other e-commerce site in conversion. You have to put great effort into maximising your listings because the place is saturated with products and most customers don't have the patience to linger too much on any products. So you have very little time to capture and hold a buyer's attention. On Amazon, there is the 'fulfilled by amazon' and also the option to fulfil it yourself. Using both platforms comes at a cost. Ensure that you read their terms and conditions and that this option is right for you before jumping into the deep end.

Maximising your listings' visibility on Amazon is more complicated than when you are trying to boost sales for your e-commerce website. A robust Amazon promotion plan should include internal and external promotions. Below are a few internal and external ways to promote your products on Amazon:

## 90.    Use SEO to optimise your listings

Using popular keywords to optimise your listings can help you attract buyers from within Amazon and buyers from other websites. Those keywords ensure that your products have a fair chance of showing up when buyers use those keywords on search engines. Competent tools like Scope and Google Keyword Planner can help you identify keywords that buyers are using to search for products.

## 91.    Use social media to share your listings

Social media can help boost sales on Amazon. A lot of people spend an inordinate amount of time across different social media platforms. The average person spends at least two hours per day online. This is an avenue to bring your products directly to customers. However, there are strategic ways to share instead of bombarding your followers with ads of your products. You could use promo codes, insert links into your content or organise a contest on your timeline.

## 92. Analyse your competition

This applies even when you're dealing with your e-commerce site. You constantly need to check your competition to see what they are doing and try to stay ahead of the curve. To improve internal visibility on Amazon, you need to know what's driving buyers to purchase the products of your competition. Few things you need to look out for include price, images and texts.

## 93. Use influencers

Influencers are those prominent figures in the African attire industry. You could get them to give your product a shout on their social media accounts. Influencers typically have large followings on their social media accounts. Having them talk about your product provides a boost, prompting people to check out your products.

## 94. Strive for higher ratings

Product ratings help Amazon keep the marketplace as competitive as possible, so try to get and maintain higher ratings. Your ratings are visible on your products and customers tend to settle for products with higher ratings. Two things that have a big pull on customers are price and ratings. To get and maintain high ratings, describe your product as it is in your listing, provide excellent customer service, and pacify disappointed buyers as best you can.

## 95.    Try lightning deals

Apart from the convenience of home delivery, buyers come to Amazon looking for reduced prices. Lightning deals appear on Amazon's Today's Deals section. These products are time-based and go for discounted prices. The fact that the products are time-based encourage customers to make purchases as quickly as possible.

For more information on e-commerce and Amazon affiliate programs, you could do a youtube search, check on udemy.com, purchase relevant books on Amazon.com or communicate with us at jacksinspiration.com.

## 96.    Utilise Data Analytics

It is important to keep and analyse statistical information. Which are the most popular products on your site? Popular sizes? Is there a trend? What colours are popular? Who are the repeat customers? Which customers regularly request a refund? In which geographical locations are your products popular? In which locations are the greatest spending? The analysis will guide your strategic decisions. Tools like Google Analytics and Hubspot Analytics come in handy here.

## 97.    Benefits of Record Keeping

Record keeping is a very important habit for business owners. Bookkeeping involves things like tax and accounting systems. Below are some of the reasons why you should keep tax and accounting records of your African attire business:

98.  **Tax saving:** When you keep up-to-date records of your business, you won't have to depend on your brain, which can be unreliable sometimes. You have the correct financial cost of running the business (plus receipts), and this means you get to pay exactly what your tax is due, nothing more and nothing less.

99.  **Helps with audit:** You'd find it very difficult during business audits without good accounting records that adequately show the expenses the business has incurred. Auditors might have to depend on their judgment.

100.  **Financial position:** Good financial records help you understand the financial position of your business so that you can act accordingly.

## 101.  Reinvesting

Strategically reinvesting some of your profits into your business has many potential benefits. Below are a few of those benefits:

102.  **Increased growth:** Reinvesting some of your profits into your business would push growth if done correctly. You need to first identify which area of the business could do with more funding. This in turn brings even more profit.

103.  **Tax benefits:** Any money you reinvest into your business is counted as a business expense and this means you won't have to pay income tax on it.

104. **New knowledge:** The first time you reinvest your profit back into the business, you might not get it right. However, you gain knowledge of which area to reinvest in next and what percentage.

105. **Insurance**

We live in an uncertain world and one sudden catastrophic event can send a booming business into the ground. There are a lot of moving parts in the African attire business and something could go wrong with logistics, or there could be damage, disappointments, lawsuits or acts of God. In situations like these, you might be required to pay compensation or out of pocket expenses. For such incidental expenses, insurance may come in handy. Different kinds of insurance could help cover unforeseen happenstances. There's the professional liability insurance, property insurance, workers compensation insurance, home-based businesses, product liability insurance and business interruption insurance. Seek advice before embarking on this.

106. **Ethics And Social Responsibility**

When doing business, it is recommended to do so ethically. Make every effort to pay what is due. And also to be fair and just with all associates. This will normally bring enduring benefits. Making profit by all and any means at the expense of others may bring initial gain, but fate generally has a way of catching up.

Additionally, we are all responsible for making the world a better place. Hopefully, when you become successful, remember to give back to society. This may be in the form of scholarships and charity, or through empowerment activities that will positively impact the communities of operation.

## 107.   Disclaimer

The opinions expressed in this ebook are those of a generalist. Those who work or study in the industry will have more technical knowledge. The whole idea of this ebook is to share thoughts on what appears to be a gap in the marketplace. You may seek more professional advice as necessary.

It is hoped that you had an open and positive mind while reading this book. The information herein is an idea that needs to be nurtured. You may come up with better ideas, or this might stimulate other ideas. As they say, the journey of a thousand miles begins with a step. I've taken the step, please continue the journey. For talks on other topics, please feel free to join our channel by searching for 'Jack Lookman' on YouTube. You can also join our Facebook group by searching Empowerment, Inspiration and Support on Facebook.com.

Ire o.

www.jacksinspiration.com